KT-375-354

I celebrated **World Book Day 2022** with this gift from my local bookseller and Farshore.

A message from World Book Day.

WORLD BOOK DAY

World Book Day's mission is to offer every child and young person the opportunity to read and love books by giving you the chance to have a book of your own.

To find out more, and for fun activities including our monthly book club, video stories and book recommendations visit **worldbookday.com**

World Book Day is a charity funded by publishers and booksellers in the UK and Ireland.

World Book Day is also made possible by generous sponsorship from National Book Tokens and support from authors and illustrators.

This book is dedicated to Terry Glossop. I don't actually know anyone of that name but nonetheless I hope if there is a Terry Glossop somewhere this will make him happy. And anyone called Vanessa Barnes or Roger Conway (who I also don't know). - M.L.

For Dora - S.H.

First published in Great Britain 2022 by Red Shed, part of Farshore
An imprint of HarperCollins*Publishers*
1 London Bridge Street, London SE1 9GF
www.farshore.co.uk

HarperCollins*Publishers*
1st Floor, Watermarque Building, Ringsend Road
Dublin 4, Ireland

Text copyright © Matt Lucas 2022
Illustrations of Matt Lucas copyright © Matt Lucas 2020, 2021, 2022
Illustrated by Sarah Horne
All other illustrations copyright © Sarah Horne 2020, 2021, 2022
Matt Lucas and Sarah Horne have asserted their moral rights.
With special thanks to Rebecca Lewis-Oakes.

ISBN 978 0 00 851983 4
Printed and bound by CPI Group (UK) Ltd, Croydon CRO 4YY.
001

A CIP catalogue record for this title is available from the British Library.

All rights reserved. No part of this publication may be reproduced, stored in a retrieval system, or transmitted, in any form or by any means, electronic, mechanical, photocopying, recording or otherwise, without the prior permission of the publisher and copyright owner.

Stay safe online. Any website addresses listed in this book are correct at the time of going to print. However, Farshore is not responsible for content hosted by third parties. Please be aware that online content can be subject to change and websites can contain content that is unsuitable for children. We advise that all children are supervised when using the internet.

MIX
Paper from
responsible sources
FSC
www.fsc.org
FSC™ C007454

This book is produced from independently certified FSC™ paper
to ensure responsible forest management.

For more information visit: www.harpercollins.co.uk/green

My Very
Very Very Very
Very Very Very
Silly Book of
TRUE OR
FALSE

MATT LUCAS

ILLUSTRATED BY SARAH HORNE

RED
SHED

hello everybody well not everybody i dont think everybody in the world is reading this i mean babies cannot read yet for instance and i doubt dogs can either (actually maybe some labradors can as they are quite brainy for a dog) but anyway hello to everybody who is reading this book and i hope you enjoy it its full of silly facts and you have to guess whether they are true or false and then you can try them out on your friends (i have five friends they are graham sally prisha and mo oh no hang on thats four sorry i am a idiot) anyway i hope you like this book and if you do there are others in the series too have fun

if anyone is reading this book and wondering where the correct grammar and punctuation are they send their apologies but they have gone on a break to whitley bay which seemed like a good idea at the time but the beach is absolutely rammed and have you seen the price of ice creams there honestly its daylight robbery

Hello These Are the Contents

HOW MANY
WILL YOU
GET RIGHT?

ASTONISHING ANIMALS

animals are like people except they
sometimes have more legs and say less
things which is good in my view because
my mum never stops talking

A group of zebras is
called a crossing.

TRUE OR FALSE?

turn the page
to find the
answer

★ FALSE.

A group of zebras is
actually called a dazzle.

A group of cats is called a glare.
A group of rhinos is called a crash.
A group of bats is called a cauldron.

Spooky!

i wonder if
a group of teachers is
called a bore ha ha

Penguins cannot fly.
TRUE OR FALSE?

my favourite penguins in order are pingu and i dont actually know any others so just pingu although he is not actually a penguin he is a animation

Herrings talk to each other by blowing bubbles from their mouths.
TRUE OR FALSE?

A crocodile can go for up to three years without eating.
TRUE OR FALSE?

HMMM?

★ **TRUE.** Penguins can't fly but, boy, can they jump! Adélie penguins can leap up to 2m - that's higher than a tall man!

★ **FALSE.** Herrings actually communicate by farting. **PARP!**

★ **TRUE.** Crocs stay still for long periods of time to save energy. But they prefer to chomp about 50 meals a year - that's one meal per week on average.

i saw a crocodile coming out of a department store once wearing a three piece suit and a top hat he was a snappy dresser ha ha do you get it

A leafcutter ant would win an Olympic weightlifting competition.
TRUE OR FALSE?

well i dont know about this one but if crawling into my bowl of custard and getting stuck there was a olympic event they would definitely win that every time

Parrots can learn over **1,000** human words.
TRUE OR FALSE?

★ **TRUE.** These tiny ants can lift over 50 times their own body weight. That's about the same as an adult man lifting a hippopotamus!

★ **TRUE.** A blue parakeet called Puck once learned 1,728 words. Wow! That's about the same as most four year olds know!

at school they told us that a parrot will jump on your ship and shout ahoy there me hearties and steal your treasure but i seen one in the zoo and it was just sitting minding its own business i think they get an unfair rap to be honest

Bats are the only mammals that can fly.

TRUE OR FALSE?

A hippopotamus can run faster than Usain Bolt.

TRUE OR FALSE?

The world's biggest spider is almost as big as your head!

TRUE OR FALSE?

i dont know if this is true because i just had a really long shower and i actually think my head shrunk in the wash

15

★ **TRUE.** Really? But what about flying squirrels? Nope. Flying squirrels don't really fly – they jump or glide.

★ **TRUE.** Hippos can run REALLY fast – up to 48km/h. Sprinter Usain Bolt reached a top speed of 44.72km/h when he set the current 100m world record. Would a hippo stay in its lane, do you think?!

★ **FALSE.** It's BIGGER! The Goliath birdeater spider is the size of a dinner plate. It eats birds, mice, frogs and lizards.

YUCK!

SURPRISING SPORTS

so this chapter is all about sports i know you shouldnt boast but i am so good at sports you should see me dribble with the football yes i know i should really wipe my mouth but i keep forgetting

Do you like football? Try to guess which fabulous footie facts are true or false!

In most football matches, it's the midfielders who run the furthest.

Mo Salah holds the world record for most footie goals scored in a single year.

In Germany,
CARS
enjoy playing
football.

HMMM?

★ **FALSE.** Midfielders run up to 11km each – but the referee runs even further! Refs run up to 13km in order to stay close to the ball at all times.

★ **FALSE.** Mo Salah scored a mighty 32 goals in the 2017–18 season but the record is actually held by Brazilian footie legend Pelé. He scored a whopping 127 goals in the 1959–60 season!

★ **TRUE.** Yes, really! In the German game of autoball, two cars compete to push a giant football into a giant goal.

Vroom!

Horses are faster than humans.
TRUE OR FALSE?

Long jump for horses was
once an Olympic sport.
TRUE OR FALSE?

The grass on the courts
at Wimbledon is kept
short so that **SNAKES**
can't hide in it.
TRUE OR FALSE?

well i dont know if this
is true or not but if it is
true then its no wonder they
have been sneaking in those
tickets are not cheap and they
sell out in a hot minute

★ **FALSE.** What?? OK, horses are USUALLY faster than humans - but in 2002, runner Tom Johnson won a long-distance race against a horse - by just 10 seconds!

★ **TRUE.** The 1900 Olympics in Paris featured a long jump competition for horses!

★ **TRUE.** In 1949, a player was bitten by a snake. Since then the grass is kept at just 8mm high - about the length of your fingernail.

well a horse is certainly faster than me unless it is a clothes horse ha ha because they dont move because they are not a real horse you see they are just a thing you put your clothes on ha ha oh never mind

Golf, javelin and a marathon have
all been performed in space.

TRUE OR FALSE?

TRUE. In 1971, Alan Shepard hit two golf balls on the Moon and Edgar Mitchell threw a javelin (well, sort of - he threw a lunar scoop, a tool used to collect soil samples). Astronaut Tim Peake completed the London marathon in the International Space Station in 2016. His time was 3 hours 35 minutes and 21 seconds, and he was over the Moon! Geddit?

i would like to go to space for maybe an afternoon but then i would like to come home because i dont think there are any toilets on the moon and i would probably need a wee by then

Can you spot which sporting origins are true or false?

 The Olympics were invented in Olympia.

 Orienteering was invented in Leyton Orient.

Rugby was invented in Rugby.

Bowling was invented in Boulder, Colorado.

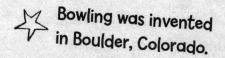

did you know the british spelling of colorado is colourado ha ha its not but it should be

★ **TRUE.** The first Olympic Games were held in Olympia in ancient Greece.

★ **FALSE.** Orienteering was invented in Sweden (and Leyton Orient is a football club, not a place!).

★ **TRUE.** Rugby was invented in Rugby, England.

★ **FALSE.** Bowling was invented around 3200BCE in Egypt.

FLABBERGASTING FOOD

this bit is all about food i love food
so much i have some every day one fact
about food that is not in this chapter is
that food was named after the inventor
of food doctor ian food in 1986
ha ha not really

A man once ate an entire aeroplane.

TRUE OR FALSE?

TRUE. Wow! Yes, really! Frenchman Michel Lotito, nicknamed Monsieur Mangetout ('Mr Eat-Everything') ate lots of strange things, including beds, bicycles and a WHOLE PLANE, cut into small pieces. It took him two years. Hmm. Crunchy!

i hope he didnt eat it for his inflight meal or there would have been no plane left and they would have had to go back home again very quickly before they fell

Pumpkins are not vegetables.
TRUE OR FALSE?

Strawberries are not berries.
TRUE OR FALSE?

Peanuts are nuts.
TRUE OR FALSE?

★ **TRUE.** A pumpkin has seeds, so it's actually a fruit!

★ **TRUE.** Yes, really! Raspberries and blackberries aren't berries either - but tomatoes and bananas ARE. It's all berry bizarre!

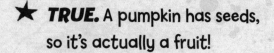

ok my head is spinning now if strawberries are not berries and they are not straw then what are they

★ **FALSE.** Peanuts aren't nuts OR fruit OR vegetables. They are actually 'legumes'.

im sorry but if peanuts are not nuts and they are not peas then i QUIT

The first food eaten on the Moon
was a cheese and pickle sandwich.

TRUE OR FALSE?

In Spain, people throw tomatoes
at each other for fun.

TRUE OR FALSE?

Bread, potatoes and
bananas have all been
used for predicting
the future.

TRUE OR FALSE?

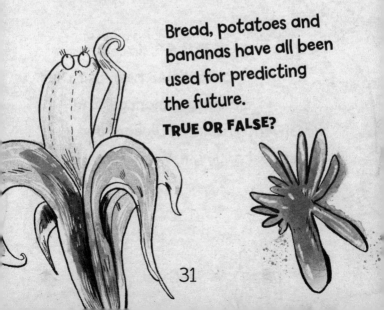

★ **FALSE.** In fact, the first meal on the Moon was tinned peaches, bacon squares and sugar cookie cubes. Astronauts Neil Armstrong and Buzz Aldrin were the first to eat (and walk!) on the Moon in 1969.

★ **TRUE.** This is during a festival called Tomatina, celebrated every August. Splat!

★ **FALSE.** However – cheese HAS been used. It's called tyromancy – and was invented over 500 years ago. No, I'm not saying it WORKS . . .

Carrots help you
to see at night.
TRUE OR FALSE?

carrots dont help you to sea
unless you are in a boat made
from carrots ha ha oh sorry
its see i thought it said sea my
mistake ignore that

FALSE. Surprised? Me too! Carrots are full of vitamin A, which is good for your eyes, but they don't help you see in the dark! It's a MYTH that started during World War Two. The British Royal Air Force had a new invention called 'radar' that helped them locate enemy positions at night. They wanted to keep it top secret so they started the rumour that British soldiers were eating LOADS of carrots and hitting more targets because of their amazing night vision!

TERRIFIC TRAVEL

now it is time for some facts about travel
my favourite way to travel is the jetpack
i havent been on one yet but if i could i
would use it to fly up to the roof of my
house and hide so when my mum comes
in to tell me to tidy my room there
would be no one there ha ha

The first bicycle was pulled by a horse.
TRUE OR FALSE?

The first speeding car was slower than a bicycle.
TRUE OR FALSE?

Scotland's Forth Bridge is soooo long that once they've painted it, they need to start at the other end again.
TRUE OR FALSE?

i once been to scotland everyone kept going on and on about the edinburgh tattoo so i went to see it and it was weird nobody actually had a tattoo there was just some people marching what a con

London Bridge is actually in Arizona, USA.

TRUE OR FALSE?

★ **FALSE.** The first bicycle was called a 'draisine' and it had wheels, but no pedals. It was invented so that people could get around WITHOUT a horse. Sorry, Sugarlump!

i told my sister my bike is made of spaghetti and she didnt believe me until i rode pasta ha ha not really its a joke silly

★ **TRUE.** In 1896, the first ever speeding ticket was given to Walter Arnold for doing 13km/h on a 3km/h road in Kent. A policeman easily caught up with him by bicycle! Cars were so new that you had to have someone walking in front with a red flag to warn people to get out of the way!

FALSE. People say this a lot – but it isn't true! The Forth Bridge is 2.6km long and takes about ten years to paint. BUT the painters used special paint that should last for 25 years!

★ **TRUE.** The original London Bridge was sold because it was falling down (just like the rhyme – yes, really!). It was moved to Arizona brick by brick in 1968. Sadly the buyer was disappointed: he thought he was buying Tower Bridge, which was much fancier! Oops.

The Great Wall of China is
the only man-made object
you can see from space.

TRUE OR FALSE?

Queen Elizabeth II is not
allowed a passport.

TRUE OR FALSE?

i saw a documentary about the great wall of china on tv not being funny it didnt look that great there werent any rollercoasters or shops or cinemas there or anything it was a bit boring they should just call it the ok wall of china

★ **FALSE.** You can see bridges, airports, large roads and city lights at night. Actually the Great Wall of China is really hard to spot - it's surrounded by rocks the exact same colour!

★ **FALSE.** She just doesn't need one! All UK passports are issued in her name, so she doesn't have to give herself permission to travel. Good thing - she's visited over 110 countries!

The Eiffel Tower has the
highest toilets in Europe.
TRUE OR FALSE?

did you know
that the eiffel tower
was named after the man
who designed it john tower
ha ha not really its
a joke

In Australia, sharks swim
through the streets.
TRUE OR FALSE?

☆

France has six villages
called Silly.
TRUE OR FALSE?

43

★ **FALSE.** Europe's highest loo is actually on the slopes of the mountain Mont Blanc. You can poo a whopping 4,260m up!

★ **TRUE.** Well, not all the time – but it did happen! It once rained so much in Ipswich, south east Queensland, that sharks swam out of the flooded river and into the streets. **YIKES!**

eek i hope i dont meet a shark in the park especially after dark it might leave a mark

★ **TRUE.** There are six villages called Trécon, which means 'silly' in French. And there are 12 villages called Billy as well!

EXTRAORDINARY ENTERTAINMENT

this chapter is all about films and
tv programmes and things like that
my favourite tv show is the news i have
every episode ever on dvd ha ha not really

In 2010, there
was a special
concert just
for dogs.
TRUE OR FALSE?

★ **TRUE.** Hundreds of dogs came to listen to a special concert outside the Sydney Opera House in Australia. Calming music was played at a frequency only dogs could hear!

apparently the concert was free but people were invited to give a small dalmation to charity

An American art gallery once
exhibited an ordinary apple
taped to the wall.

TRUE OR FALSE?

A French artist called Aquabouse
paints portraits using cow dung.

TRUE OR FALSE?

In Austria, there is an
orchestra where all the
instruments are rocks.

TRUE OR FALSE?

In Jurassic Park, dinosaurs
only appear onscreen for
a total of 30 minutes.

TRUE OR FALSE?

well i am peachless this sounds most apeeling and like a berry good way of raisin a melon pounds

★ **FALSE.** It was actually a banana, and it sold for £87,000 in 2019!

★ **TRUE.** And guess what he paints using cow dung? COWS!

★ **FALSE.** The truth is even sillier. The instruments are all vegetables! They include carrot recorders, radish flutes and pumpkin drums.

★ **FALSE.** Dinos star for only 15 mins! That's not a lot of roar!

i saw jurassic park and it was quite scary you have to admit those dinosaurs are good actors

Films are great, aren't they. But actors and directors aren't the only people working on a film set. Can you spot which jobs are real and which are made-up?

Grip

Dolly Grip

Key Grip

Best Boy

Child Wrangler

Crocodile Wrangler

dolly grip sounds like one of the women my nan sits with at bingo

★ **_Grip – TRUE,_** takes care of the cameras.

★ **_Dolly Grip – TRUE,_** moves the cameras and dollies (the platforms the cameras rest on).

★ **_Key Grip – TRUE,_** in charge of all the other grips.

★ **_Best Boy – TRUE,_** helps the Key Grip. And don't worry, girls can be 'best boys' too!

★ **_Child Wrangler – TRUE,_** looks after child actors on set.

★ **_Crocodile Wrangler – FALSE,_** but on-set electricians are sometimes called Python Wranglers, because electric cables look like snakes!

Have you ever been to the theatre? Behind the scenes there are lots of traditions and sayings - but which are true?

☆ Saying 'good luck' is bad luck in the theatre.

☆ It's bad luck to sneeze in a theatre.

☆ You must always leave a light on the stage to scare away the ghosts.

i love acting and i also love animals i once put on a play for some cows but they didnt like it and i got mooed off

★ **TRUE.** Saying 'good luck' in the theatre is considered to be bad luck. Actors always say 'break a leg' instead!

★ **FALSE.** Everyone needs to sneeze sometimes! However it's not a good idea to whistle. Theatre technicians whistle to each other before scene changes. So, if you're just whistling a happy tune, you might get a tree falling on your head!

★ **TRUE.** A light, called the 'ghost light', is always left shining onstage to ward off ghosts. Well, wouldn't you want the stage to be free of spooks?

i dont believe in ghosts its absolute nonsense apart from one i seen in a film

OH-SO YUCKY!

this is the yuckiest chapter in the book so you have been warned actually it is so yucky you may want to open a window and hold your nose while you read it

Elephants do **50kg of poo** a day.
TRUE OR FALSE?

★ **FALSE.** It's more! Much more! African elephants poo up to 110kg* of poo every day! They eat about 140kg of food, though, so that's less silly. I'm glad I'm not a zookeeper.

*That's about the same weight as a Giant Panda.

well that is a lot of poo i hate to think how much a elephant spends on air freshener

You can sneeze in your sleep.
TRUE OR FALSE?

You can fart in your sleep.
TRUE OR FALSE?

You can poo in your sleep.
TRUE OR FALSE?

> i wonder if when a nut sneezes it says 'cashew'

★ **FALSE.** The bit of your brain that's needed for sneezing is also asleep!

★ **TRUE.** But you don't realise. A sleep fart would never be loud enough to wake you up.

★ **FALSE.** The body's digestive system goes to sleep at bedtime. Babies stop pooing in their sleep by about four months old, then that's it – poo stays inside!.

z z z

Cows fart enough
to fill 44 billion
balloons every day.
TRUE OR FALSE?

Turtles can breathe out
of their bums and wee
out of their mouths.
TRUE OR FALSE?

Crushed-up Egyptian mummies
were used to cure bruises.
TRUE OR FALSE?

★ **TRUE.** There are about one billion cows on Earth, and each cow produces about 500 litres of methane (aka fart gas) every day from burps, farts and poo. Enough to fill 44 billion balloons.

★ **TRUE.** The Chinese soft-shelled turtle is the only creature alive that can wee out of its bum AND its mouth.

★ **TRUE.** In the 1500s, doctors used to give patients a drink made out of ground-up mummies to cure everything from bruises to stomach ulcers.

YUCK!

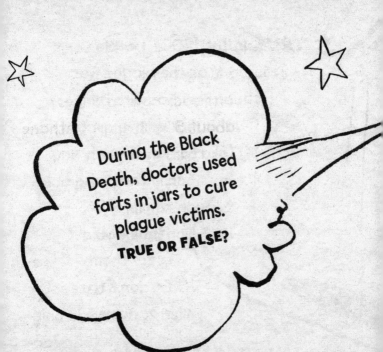

During the Black Death, doctors used farts in jars to cure plague victims.
TRUE OR FALSE?

Ancient Romans collected rain water to use as mouthwash to whiten their teeth.
TRUE OR FALSE?

★ **TRUE.** In the 1400s, people believed that the plague was caused by 'bad air'. They thought if they diluted the bad air with something else – ahem, FARTS! – that would cure them. Er, don't try this at home!

★ **FALSE.** Romans actually used something MUCH yuckier to clean their teeth:

WEE!

★ **TRUE.** This must be the worst job ever, right? The word 'stool' meant the commode or portable toilet that the king sat on to poop. The 'Groom of the Stool' made notes on what Henry ate, accompanied him to the loo and even had to wipe his bottom!

GRRRRRRR-OSSS!!

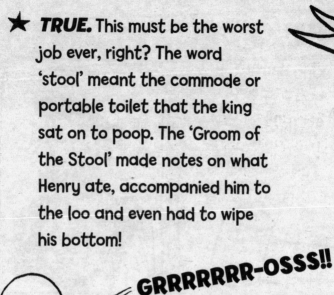

62

this bit contains facts all about people believe it or not i actually met some real people once dont ask me what they were like i cant remember i was very young at the time

You are just as hairy as a chimpanzee.

TRUE OR FALSE?

★ **TRUE.** Humans have about the same number of hairs on our bodies as chimps and other apes! We all have five MILLION hair follicles – the bit the hair grows out of. A lot of our hair is so fine and wispy that it can't be seen – so humans rarely LOOK as hairy as chimps!

i love chimpanzees and did you know a flying monkey is called a hot air baboon ha not really a flying monkey would be cool apart from if it stole your tv aerial which it could do as they are quite naughty sometimes

Children grow faster
in the autumn.
TRUE OR FALSE?

Your teeth keep
growing for your
whole life.
TRUE OR FALSE?

Over half your
body is **NOT**
human.
TRUE OR FALSE?

WOOF

★ **FALSE.** Children grow fastest in the spring. You also grow faster when you're asleep than when you're awake.

★ **FALSE.** Once your adult teeth appear, they stop growing. Your nose and ears never stop growing though! Yes . . . you heard that right!

★ **TRUE.** Yes! So weird! Human cells make up only 10-43% of the body. The rest is billions and billions of bacteria, fungi and viruses. Ew!

my teeth are lovely
in fact my dentist is so good
they put a plaque on his wall
and he just scraped it off
ha ha

Just 1% of people in the world have red hair.

TRUE OR FALSE?

☆

Only 10% of British people have blue eyes.

TRUE OR FALSE?

☆

Britons are taller today than they were in the past.

TRUE OR FALSE?

> i used to have red hair except it was yellow

★ **TRUE.** Red hair is slightly more common in Scotland and Ireland than in England and Wales, and it's way more common in Europe than on other continents.

★ **FALSE.** 48% of Britons have blue eyes! 30% have green eyes and 22% have brown eyes. Globally about 90% have brown eyes, 8% blue and 2% green. What colour are your eyes?

★ **TRUE.** Brits get taller by an average of 2cm with every new generation!

Can you tell which of these fascinating family facts is true?

The Duke family from the USA were the first family to travel to the Moon.

The biggest family in the world would fill Wembley Stadium more than twice.

★ **FALSE.** Astronaut Charles Duke was the tenth person to walk on the Moon in 1972, but his family DIDN'T go with him. Someone had to stay home and look after the dog – probably? But Charles did leave a photo of his family on the Moon's surface – and it's still there today!

★ **TRUE.** The Långaryd family of Sweden claims to be the world's biggest family, with 190,000 known members – that's 2% of Sweden's entire population!

guess how many tottenham fans you could fit in wembley stadium ... we will never know because they will never get there ha i am only joking they will get there one day but they will lose because the other team are better

Dwayne 'The Rock' Johnson and his dad, Rocky Johnson, were both WWF wrestling champions.

TRUE OR FALSE?

Alex Oxlade-Chamberlain and his dad, Mark Chamberlain, are world-champion divers.

TRUE OR FALSE?

The Williams sisters - Venus, Serena and Janice - hold the record for most tennis Grand Slam titles of any sisters: 25 singles and 13 doubles.

TRUE OR FALSE?

i am really good at tennis apart from the bit where you have to hit the ball back over the net but otherwise i am really good at it i like wrestling because when someone sits on you you can have a nice rest

★ **TRUE.** Before The Rock was a huge movie star, he won four world championships and five tag team championships. His dad, Rocky, was also a national champ!

★ **FALSE.** They're footie legends! Mark played for Stoke, Portsmouth and represented England eight times. Alex moved from Arsenal to Liverpool and has already played for England 35 times!

★ **FALSE.** Only Venus and Serena are sisters. But it's TRUE they hold all those titles!

STUPENDOUS SCIENCE

some of the facts in this chapter are about inventions if i could invent anything i would invent a lemon that tastes completely of orange and it would be the same shape as a orange and the colour of it would be orange too

A day is longer than a
year on the planet Venus.
TRUE OR FALSE?

The first frisbees were
overcooked pies.
TRUE OR FALSE?

i like pork pies and i
like blueberry pies but
once i made a pork
and blueberry pie and
it was poo m'loo

i bought a hoover but i am taking it back to the shop because it sucks ha ha it is a joke

A man called Hoover invented the first vacuum cleaner.

TRUE OR FALSE?

Right now, **3.6 billion** people are using the internet.

TRUE OR FALSE?

★ **TRUE.** I know - whaaat?! Venus takes 243 Earth days to spin on its axis, which is longer than it takes to travel around the Sun (225 Earth days). Other mind-boggling facts: a day on Jupiter only lasts ten hours, while a year on Neptune lasts 165 (Earth) years!

★ **FALSE.** But it's ALMOST true! In the 1940s, William Russell Frisbee, a baker, started printing his name, 'Frisbee', on the tins he made his pies in. Some silly students started throwing the Frisbee tins . . . and discovered they flew REALLY well!

76

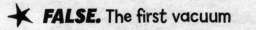 **FALSE.** The first vacuum cleaner was built by Hubert Cecil Booth and was SO big it had to be pulled around by a horse-drawn cart. William Henry Hoover ran a company that sold vacuum cleaners ... which eventually became known as hoovers. Well, that's cleaned up that one!

TRUE. Well, give or take one or two! That's over half the world's population. Are you online right now? NO, you're reading this AWESOME BOOK!

> i wonder how long it would take you to read the whole of the internet at least an afternoon i reckon especially if you include all of google

Which phone facts are phoney? Geddit?!

The first mobile phone weighed 1.1kg (that's the same as three tins of baked beans).

Nomophobia is the fear of phones.

Mobile phones are dirtier than toilet handles.

In Finland, it's illegal to drop a mobile phone.

★ ***TRUE.*** And it cost almost £3,000! Yikes!

★ ***FALSE.*** Nomophobia is actually the fear of NOT having your phone with you!

★ ***TRUE.*** We use them all day but we don't clean them much. In fact, a phone has 18 times more bacteria than a loo handle.

GRRR-OSS!

★ ***FALSE.*** That would be silly! In fact, Finland invented a sport called Phone Throwing. The world championship is held every year and the record throw is over 100m. Don't try this at home!

HAIR-RAISING HISTORY

this bit is all about history which is
things that happened in the past but
some of these things didnt happen and
you have to guess if they did or not
one thing that definitely happened in the
past was when i was a baby and i done
a poo in the bath but i think probably the
historical things in this chapter are
a bit more important than that at least
i hope they are because i dont
want anyone to find out

When Charles Darwin travelled
on the HMS Beagle, he took a
beagle with him for good luck.
TRUE OR FALSE?

FALSE. Famous naturalist Charles Darwin loved dogs but he didn't take a beagle on the *Beagle*! Dogs have never been considered lucky on ships – unlike cats, which sailors have often taken on their voyages to bring good luck (and to catch rats and mice!). When Charles Darwin set off on the HMS Beagle in 1831 – travelling the world to discover more about its creatures and their habitats – his dogs stayed at home!

The Great Fire of
London began in
a blacksmith's on
Forge Street.
TRUE OR FALSE?

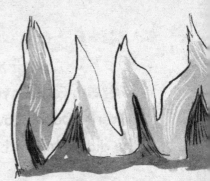

During World War Two, a reindeer
lived on a submarine for six weeks.
TRUE OR FALSE?

it depends whether
its father christmas's
submarine i guess but then i dont
know if he has a submarine or not
i only know he has a sleigh to deliver
presents and maybe a mobility scooter
for the rest of the time as he is
quite old now you know

★ **FALSE.** It actually started in a bakery on Pudding Lane. Someone's buns got very burnt!

★ **TRUE.** A reindeer called Pollyanna was given as a gift to the submarine HMS *Trident* by the Soviet navy. Pollyanna stayed on board for six weeks till they got home to the UK, then she went to live at London Zoo.

King Henry III had a pet polar bear.
TRUE OR FALSE?

The horns on Vikings' helmets were used for drinking while on the move.
TRUE OR FALSE?

ive heard that the vikings were very aggressive so i think if i went hiking or biking with the viking high king it would probably not be to my liking

★ **TRUE.** Wouldn't you like a pet polar bear? Lots of kings and queens kept unusual pets. King Henry I had lions, camels and even porcupines. George III owned a cheetah and Queen Victoria had two Tibetan mountain goats.

★ **FALSE.** Vikings never actually had horns on their helmets – it's a myth. But they DID sometimes drink out of horns!

Martin Luther King was named
after a German monk who lived
over 500 years ago.
TRUE OR FALSE?

You drink the same water
as the dinosaurs.
TRUE OR FALSE?

In ancient China, kings
and queens kept dogs
up their sleeves.
TRUE OR FALSE?

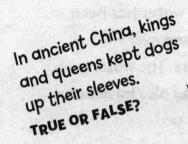

i really am not
sure about this one but
if I had to take a guess
i would say it is either
true or false

★ **TRUE.** Martin Luther King, the Civil Rights activist, was originally named Michael King. Michael's dad renamed himself and his son after visiting the birthplace of Martin Luther, a famous monk and religious reformer.

★ **TRUE.** Earth's water has been recycled over and over for four billion years. The water you drink today may also have been slurped by a T. rex!

★ **TRUE.** The dogs were ready to jump out and scare anyone who wanted to attack their royal owners.

WOOF!

THE SILLIEST TRUE OR FALSE IN THE WORLD

the silliest fact in this whole book is on the next page it is sooooooo silly it is sillier even than a teapot made of chocolate

The first garden gnomes were real people.
TRUE OR FALSE?

Bonkers, right? Well, rich people in the 1700s didn't have telly or anything like that so they spent a LOT of time in their gardens. In fact, they competed with their friends to see who had the best, most exciting one. They added all sorts of things like lakes, bridges and secret gardens. THEN someone had the idea to build a small 'grotto' or cave, and pay someone to live there – real, live gnomes!

Sounds like a fun job? Not really! Being a gnome – or 'ornamental hermit' – meant living in your small grotto **ALL THE TIME.**

They weren't allowed to leave the garden and some 'gnomes' weren't allowed to speak – in order to appear mysterious and magical! Would you agree to be a gnome for extra pocket money?!

well i hope you enjoyed this very very very very very very very silly book and if you did you may like to know you can also read my very very very very very very very silly book of jokes my very very very very very very very silly book of pranks and my very very very very very very very silly book of games well bye then hope you have a nice day or night if it is night and remember KEEP IT SILLY

WORLD **BOOK** DAY
3 MARCH 2022

Happy
World Book Day!

As a charity, our mission is to encourage every child and young person to enjoy reading, and to have a book of their own.

> Everyone is a reader — that includes you!

Whether you enjoy **comics**, **fact books**, **adventure stories**, **recipes** – books are for everyone and every book counts.

On **World Book Day**, everyone comes together to have **FUN** reading. Talking about and sharing books with your friends and family makes reading even more memorable and magic.

World Book Day™ is a registered charity sponsored by National Book Tokens.

NATION. **BOO** toker

Illustration by Allen Fatimaharan © 2021

Where will your **reading journey** take you next?

1 Take a trip to your local bookshop

Brimming with brilliant books and helpful booksellers to share awesome reading recommendations, bookshops are magical places. You can even enjoy booky events and meet your favourite authors and illustrators!

Find your nearest bookseller at booksaremybag.com/Home

2 Join your local library

A world awaits you in your local library – that place where all the books you could ever want to read await. Even better, you can borrow them for **FREE**! Libraries can offer expert advice on what to read next, as well as free family reading events.

Find your local library at gov.uk/local-library-services

Scan here to visit our website!

3 Check out the World Book Day website

Looking for reading tips, advice and inspiration? There is so much to discover at worldbookday.com/getreading, packed with book recommendations, fun activities, audiobooks, and videos to enjoy on your own or as a family, as well as competitions and all the latest book news galore.

World Book Day® is a registered charity sponsored by National Book Tokens.

Illustration by Allen Fatimaharan © 2021

NATIONAL
BOOK
tokens

Matt Lucas

MATT LUCAS is an actor, writer, comedian and very silly person. He became famous by playing a big baby in a crazy TV show called *Shooting Stars*. His next TV show was called *Little Britain*, which he did with David Walliams. *Little Britain* was very rude indeed and you are not allowed to watch it until you are at least 75 years old.

Recently Matt has been presenting on *The Great British Bake Off* and also writing and singing about his friend, Baked Potato.

Sarah Horne

SARAH HORNE is an illustrator and writer. She first learned to draw aged nine, when she needed to explain to the hairdresser how she wanted her hair to be cut. The result was not what she had hoped for – but her picture was pretty amazing.

Since then, Sarah's drawing (and haircuts) have got even better. She has illustrated over 70 (mostly) very silly books.